The Gem of Protection

The Ageless Gem Series
Book 2

Raeann Gillberg

Relax. Read. Repeat.

THE GEM OF PROTECTION (The Ageless Gem Series, Book 2)
By Raeann Gillberg
Published by TouchPoint Press
Brookland, AR 72417
www.touchpointpress.com

Copyright © 2022 Raeann Gillberg
All rights reserved.

Softcover ISBN: 978-1-956851-53-3
Hardcover ISBN: 978-1-956851-54-0

Editor: Jenn Haskin
Cover Design: ColbieMyles.com

Cover Images: Great Wall of China, watercolor; yellow amber gem isolated, topaz (Shutterstock)

Interior Images: (Adobestock) A stack of books to read by ozrolf; Great Wall of China, XIX century engraving by acrogame; Hand drawn sketch of Great Wall of China isolated by fuzzylogickate; The Great Wall of China in sketch style. Illustration, hand drawn, sketch isolated on white. Watercolor by Evgenia; Snowflake isolated on white background by Alexey Kljatov (Shutterstock) Emperor buried in the pits next to the Qin Shi Huang's of China. The Terracotta Army or the "Terra Cotta Warriors and Horses" 2,000 years. portrait on 1 Lunar Dollars 2017 Banknote.

First Edition

Printed in the United States of America.

Thank you to my amazing family, friends, and teachers who have supported me and my book.

1: The Great Wall of China

Thou who shall find the Gem of Age, shall be young, but one of the chosen ones no doubt. There shall be two gem masters, and only they can truly use the gems. Till they grow old, and the gems are passed down to the four, and the four shall unlock the true potential in the gems.

The words of the prophecy came back to Lilly as she was deep in thought. Lilly sighed as she tried to sleep. Her mind was obviously too busy to sleep right now, so she might as well read a bit more.

Over the past few months, Lilly had decided to read all she could about ancient places with great historical value. After getting the *Ageless Gem* over the summer, she and Peter had learned that they would have to collect the gems from around the world. She knew that if they were to find all the gems, then they would have to research places they might be hidden.

Peter seemed to think that searching about the gems on the internet was a better idea than actually reading books about the possible locations for the gem. However, Lilly didn't think the internet was the most reliable source of information, so she didn't pay much attention to what Peter claimed to have found during his 5-minute internet search.

So far, Lilly had learned a lot about historical landmarks, but she hadn't found out a lot about the gems. She had only found vague theories about where the gems might be hidden. However, there was no record of anyone having found them, so they were often considered to be nothing more than a myth. Despite this, Lilly knew that the gems were real.

After all, Lilly and Peter found the *Ageless*

Gem last summer in Petra, guarded by a tyrannosaurus-rex, and assorted traps. But they also met a scientist named Brian who was also after the gems. Which meant they would have to be careful, not only of Brian but also of whatever was guarding the gems.

The next day was all hustle and bustle, as they loaded the car with their luggage. They were going to visit the Great Wall of China for her dad's work. He was writing articles on the seven wonders of the world in our modern time, and how tourism has impacted them. However, Lilly and Peter planned to use the opportunity that these trips provided to search for the gems at each of the seven wonders of the world.

Soon they were on their way to the airport. There they boarded a plane. During the plane ride, Lilly tapped Peter's shoulder to get his attention.

"What?" asked Peter.

"Are you super excited or what?" Lilly asked excitedly. Peter smiled at Lilly as she recalled that when they went to Petra during the summer, Peter had been having strange dreams, which helped them find the gem. "Also, I wanted to know if you've had any dreams, like last time."

"No," answered Peter. "No dreams this time. Why don't you just read your books about The Great Wall of China?"

Just then a flight attendant walked by to ask if they needed anything. They both politely declined. After she left it didn't seem like Peter wanted to talk anymore, so Lilly decided to take a nap since she didn't get very much sleep the previous night.

Soon Lilly drifted off into a strange dream. *In front of her, stretched a long wall, so long she couldn't see the end. Even though this was true, she knew what wall this was, The Great Wall of China. Lilly recalled from her books that The Great Wall of China was 21,196 kilometers long, or 13,170 miles. It stretched across China's northern border and was built by China's first emperor, Qin Shi Huang, to keep out invaders.*

Lilly's dream took her to a part of the wall where a person was walking, but Lilly couldn't tell who it was. The person then turned around and Lilly instantly recognized who it was. It was Brian—he was after the gem that was at The Great Wall of China, too!

Lilly and Peter would have to hurry if they wanted to get to the gem before him.

2: Breakfast

The next day Lilly told Peter about her dream as they were getting breakfast in the hotel lobby. The buffet offered foods that Lilly had never seen before, as well as some she was used to seeing. There were donuts, waffles, and muffins, as well as rice, and other things Lilly didn't know the name of.

"What's this?" asked Peter, putting something that resembled an extra fluffy pancake onto his plate. Lilly shook her head. She hadn't thought to do any research on the food before they came, since it didn't seem like an important topic to research.

"Why don't you try it and find out?" said

Lilly, as she debated getting what looked like some kind of lumpy milk.

"There's a sign here," said Peter. "Egg pancakes. What are egg pancakes?"

Lilly shook her head as she noticed that there were signs by the food options that were in both Chinese and English. Lilly checked the sign near her, rice porridge. Lilly had no idea what rice porridge was.

"Too bad they don't have any chocolate chip pancakes," said Peter, as he grabbed a dough stick. Lilly decided to get one too, and then the two of them went to find a table to eat. Their mom waved them over to where they were sitting.

"Are we going to a museum, as we did for Petra?" asked Lilly, as they started eating.

"No," said her mom. "We're going to the Huanghuacheng section of the wall today. Besides, we have our own little information center right here. You already know way more than the rest of us." This was true, Lilly could recall plenty of facts about The Great Wall of China, so she probably wouldn't learn much from a museum.

Except, maybe more about the gem. Lilly knew so much about The Great Wall of China, but hardly anything about the gem they were supposed to find. All she knew was that it was somewhere inside the wall.

"Where are we going tomorrow?" Lilly asked out of curiosity.

"We're going to the Badaling section of the wall tomorrow," answered her mom, between sips of coffee.

"Both of you need to stay close and not wander off like you did at Petra," said their dad. "We might not be able to find you if you wander off again, and then what would you do?"

"End up lost in a foreign country with no hope of ever getting home," said Peter sarcastically. This was a conversation they'd had a few times.

Their parents were very upset after they disappeared when they were visiting Petra. Lilly doubted it would be as easy to sneak away to retrieve the gem this time, but she would have to find the gem first.

3: New Facts

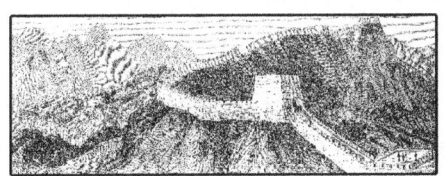

In the distance, Lilly could see the wall coming into view. As they got closer, Lilly saw why people called it "The Great Wall." It was enormous. It was evident that the wall would have been able to protect the country from many invaders.

"It must have taken them a long time to build that wall," said her mom.

"Well, the original Great Wall of China took

 about 20 years to construct, while the one you can see today took around 2,000 years," recalled Lilly.

Lilly watched as delicate snowflakes fell onto the wall, covering it in a white blanket. A crisp cold wind blew across the wall making her shiver from its bone-chilling touch.

"I thought it was supposed to be summer here," said Peter.

"Why did you think it would be summer?" asked Lilly. "It's winter back home."

"Well," began Peter. "We are on the opposite side of the world. Isn't it supposed to be the opposite season?"

"Are we above or below the equator?" asked Lilly.

"Above, why?" asked Peter.

"Do we live above or below the equator?" asked Lilly, ignoring him.

"Above, but why does it matter if we live above or below the equator?" asked Peter.

"You see," began Lilly. "As the earth orbits

the sun, different parts get more sunlight than others. This creates the seasons."

"I still don't see what this has to do with the equator," said Peter.

"As you know the earth is tilted on its axis," said Lilly. "This tilt causes the opposite halves of the earth, the northern and southern hemispheres, to experience different amounts of exposure to sunlight."

"Look at you," said their mom. "Little miss smarty-pants. Teaching us all something new."

Peter rolled his eyes. "So, that means it's summer in all places below the equator, and winter above then?"

"Exactly," answered Lilly.

When they found their tour group, Lilly remembered their tour guide from a few months ago. She had been their tour guide at both the Petra Museum and Petra itself. However, their tour guide this time was different. He was a Chinese man with a blue snow coat, and he was holding a flag.

As they began the tour Lilly listened intently,

while keeping a sharp eye out for any clues about the gem. However, the tour didn't offer much information, so near the end of the tour Lilly asked the tour guide what he knew about the *Great Gems,* and about one being hidden at the Great Wall of China.

"I don't know much about them," answered the tour guide. "I have heard about the *Gem of Protection* being in the Great Wall of China."

"Do you have any idea as to where it might be hidden?" asked Lilly.

"The place that most seem to think is the Badaling section. It was the most likely way to the capital, and one of the best-preserved sections of the wall," answered the tour guide. "Though those are just theories I've heard from others."

"Isn't that where we're going tomorrow?" asked Peter.

"It is," said their mom.

Lilly smiled. This was perfect!

4: The Terracotta Soldier

Lilly didn't learn much more information the rest of the day. She was really hoping to find out more about the gems, but all she found out was stuff that confirmed what she already knew. The part about "the four" still puzzled her, however, she didn't have quite enough information to figure out that part.

As Lilly lay down for bed, she just couldn't take her mind off of the gems, and all the other things related to them. Which was why it's no wonder that she had another dream.

Lilly saw bricks all around her with stone arch windows looking out upon the snowy landscape below. Lilly figured that she must be inside one of the old guard towers on The Great Wall of China. Standing in front of her was a stone Chinese soldier in ancient battle armor. She remembered that these were called terracotta soldiers and were originally constructed for the tomb of China's first emperor. They were thought to be his army, to help him fight battles in the afterlife.

No two terracotta soldiers looked exactly alike, and they usually guarded important things, such as the first emperor's tomb. However, Lilly hadn't heard about any terracotta soldiers being found on the wall.

"Hello, young master," said the terracotta soldier in a deep voice. "I shall await your arrival."

"What?" asked Lilly, very confused about what he said, and even more about him talking at all.

"You must hurry," continued the soldier, ignoring her question. "Time is running out."

"What do you mean time is running out?" asked Lilly. However, she was already waking up.

5: The Plan

The next day, Lilly told Peter about her dream as their parents were looking over a map. It was then that Lilly noticed his shirt, which had a terracotta soldier on it.

"Where'd you get that shirt?" asked Lilly.

"Why?" asked Peter.

"It reminds me of the terracotta soldier I was telling you about," said Lilly.

"Well, that terracotta soldier sounds a lot like the t-rex from last year," said Peter. "With the whole appearing in dreams and on shirts."

Lilly nodded, she remembered the tyrannosaurus-rex. That's because it wasn't just in Peter's dreams. It had also been protecting the gem. Now, a few months later, Lilly was having a dream about a terracotta soldier.

Lilly hoped that the terracotta soldier was the same as the tyrannosaurus-rex, which meant it was nice to the gem masters, but would protect the gem from others. That would be very helpful to them, but they needed a way to retrieve the gem without anyone noticing.

"We could sneak away again," suggested Peter, interrupting her thoughts.

"But Mom and Dad would be worried again if we both disappeared," said Lilly.

"Then what if you go look for the gem, while I distract them?" suggested Peter.

"Depends on what you plan to do," said Lilly.

"Sometime during the tour, you can signal me, and I'll distract everyone," said Peter.

"That might work," said Lilly hesitantly, but before she could ask him what he planned to do, their parents were done looking over the map.

"Come on, you two," said their mom.

When they found their tour group Lilly was

very surprised at who their tour guide was. She was about average height with jet black hair and was wearing a purple winter coat with matching purple pants. She had black snow boots, magenta mittens, and a turquoise beanie to pull it all together.

"Well, if it isn't my favorite inquisitor," said Becky, noticing them.

They had met Becky last summer at Petra, where she had been their tour guide at both the museum and the actual place.

"What are you doing here?" asked Lilly, surprised. "I thought you worked at Petra."

"I've always wanted to see the seven wonders of the world," said Becky, after a second. "So, I decided to become a tour guide. Now I don't only get to see these amazing places, but I also get to teach other people about them."

"That's cool," said their dad. "Where are you going next?"

"I'm thinking somewhere warmer than here," said Becky. "But you guys are also going to see all the seven wonders of the world. Where are you guys going next?"

"We're going to Machu Picchu in the spring," said their mom.

"I'll see you there," said Becky. "Now I better get this tour started."

6: Distraction

As the tour got underway Lilly was, as always, paying close attention and asking lots of questions. The Badaling section of the Great Wall of China was supposedly the busiest section, and mostly locals visited this section of the wall. Though due to the frigid weather, there weren't as many people. That's not to say there wasn't still a crowd though.

Lilly was becoming worried about how she would be able to retrieve the gem with so many people around, and without anyone noticing. However, that meant she would have to find the gem first.

Lilly wasn't learning much about the gem through the tour either, so she was starting to get worried. However, as they passed through one of the guardhouses, Lilly felt a strange feeling. It was as if something was "off" with the air; as if it was hiding something.

"This is one of the guardhouses along the wall," said Becky as she led their tour through the guardhouse. "As you can see there are windows that look down at the beautiful landscape below, so make sure to take lots of pictures and consider coming back during the spring and summer months when the landscape is filled with lush green plants."

As the tour group moved on Lilly let Peter

know that it was time. Peter nodded, and whispered, "Be careful."

With this, Lilly started to slip to the back of the group. When they were farther away from the guardhouse Peter fell down with a loud cry. Suddenly there was a commotion as Peter seemed to have slipped and gotten hurt, however, Lilly didn't stick around to watch and quickly headed back to the guardhouse. She hoped to be back before anyone noticed her absence.

7: The Gem of Protection

Lilly made her way back to the guardhouse as quickly as possible without raising any suspicion. However, along the way, doubt started to creep into her mind. What if she was wrong and the gem wasn't hidden in the guardhouse? What if it wasn't even at the Badaling section of the wall? What if Peter had wasted his distraction for nothing?

Lilly shook her head. It was too late to turn back on her decision, so she had to believe that she was right. She had been right about the gems being real in the first place.

When Lilly reached the guardhouse, she

once again felt that something was slightly off. Looking around, she didn't see anything that looked different about the guardhouse. No, looking closely at one corner, the air seemed to be slightly distorted, but not in a way that was too noticeable. There also seemed to be an odd feeling coming from the corner as well.

Lilly walked to the corner, and it felt as if she was walking through some kind of barrier. Her whole body tingled a bit, and she felt a little dizzy. Lilly jumped a bit as she almost ran into a terracotta soldier that hadn't been there a moment before.

"Welcome gem master," said the terracotta soldier in a gravelly sounding voice.

"H-hi," said Lilly, not sure what else to say. Looking at him, Lilly realized that the terracotta soldier was wearing a necklace that had a yellow gem hanging on it. The yellow gem was glowing and seemed to be the source of the strange field. There was no doubt that that was the *Gem of Protection*.

"Thank you for making haste to retrieve the

gem," said the terracotta soldier snapping her out of her thoughts. The terracotta soldier removed the necklace from around his neck and held it out to her. "I can answer any questions you may have about the gem."

"What is this space?" asked Lilly. "I wasn't able to see you before I entered the area. Wait, can other people see us?"

"None can see us," replied the terracotta soldier. "At least until you destroy this space with the gem and continue on your quest to find the next gem. As for your other question, the space we are in protects us from others' sight. No one but the gem masters can detect it, and only they can enter so easily. This is one of the powers of the *Gem of Protection*."

"Then why not just leave the gem here?" asked Lilly. "Isn't it a lot safer if I don't take the gem?"

"It may seem so, but the gems shall be needed soon," replied the terracotta soldier rather cryptically. "I shan't say more, but you must make haste now. Our world depends on you."

"So, what happens when I leave with the gem?" asked Lilly.

"I shall no longer be hidden, and shall be able to rest from my duties," replied the terracotta soldier, as if this was the obvious answer. "However, you should make haste before your absence is noticed."

"How do I use the gem?" asked Lilly, looking around and noticing that there weren't a lot of people currently in the guardhouse.

"Simply concentrate on leaving as you walk away," instructed the terracotta soldier.

"One more question," said Lilly, remembering something. "Is there a gem at Machu Picchu?"

"I do not know of where you speak," replied the terracotta soldier. "Though I can tell you the next gem is in mountains far away. Surrounded by a forest of mist. You should hurry and return now."

Lilly waited about a minute until there was no one in the guardhouse. She then took a deep breath and focused on exiting the strange field as she walked away from the terracotta soldier.

There was a tingling sensation again as Lilly did this.

Lilly turned around and saw that the terracotta soldier now seemed like a lifeless statue, except for a subtle nod of his head as if congratulating her.

8: Protection

Lilly started back toward the tour group. However, as Lilly was leaving the guardhouse she found someone familiar blocking her way.

"Well can I assume you've got the *Gem of Protection*?" asked Brian with a smile. Lilly held the gem tightly and glanced around. There was no one else in the guardhouse, or close enough to properly see anything. Where were all the people?

"If you're wondering why there is no one here, it's because I set up a distraction on the way here," said Brian, as if reading her mind. "Now be a good kid and give me the gem. Then you can run back to your tour group."

Lilly backed up, looking for a way out. If she went in the other direction, she would be running away from her tour group, and she might not be able to find her family. Not to mention that her parents would definitely notice she was gone and would be very upset. She needed a way to get past Brian, and quickly. Then Lilly remembered the gem.

Ducking behind a wall in the guardhouse she took a deep breath and tried focusing on calling forth the gem's power of protection. Lilly felt a slight tingle in her hands and saw that the gem began to glow, just as Brian was about to reach her. Suddenly she was surrounded by yellow energy in a spherical shape that pushed him back.

"When did you learn to use the gem's powers?" asked Brian, seeming a bit surprised.

"You can't have this gem either Brian," said Lilly before running right past him; the sphere knocking him out of her way.

Lilly ran in the direction the tour group was in, but as she glanced behind her she saw Brian was chasing her. He might not be able to reach her, but he could very easily see her with the glowing force field around her. This was going to be difficult to explain. Then Lilly had an idea. She slowed down and focused on the gem. She felt a tingle throughout her body, and her shield disappeared. Brian stopped running and looked around with a look of confusion.

"Don't tell me you know how to make yourself invisible too!" exclaimed Brian, looking quite upset. Lilly smiled as it appeared she had succeeded. However, she lost the shield in the process, so she would need to be careful.

Brian started walking in the direction of the tour group, and Lilly realized he still knew where she was heading. He didn't know where she was, but he knew where she was going to be, and her route to get there. Lilly walked as quietly as she could, so as not to alert him to her exact location. She also tried to avoid stepping in snow, so as not to leave any footprints. She stayed a good distance behind him too, which proved a smart idea as Brian did in fact try to grab at the air around him a few times.

Eventually, Lilly saw the group and debated just running past Brian and the rest of the distance. However, she decided that he could probably run faster than her and would notice if she ran past.

Then Lilly noticed Brian stop and pick up some snow. Lilly also stopped to see what he was doing. Brian then proceeded to throw the snow around him, and Lilly had to back up a bit to avoid the snow landing on her and giving away her location. Brian seemed quite angry that he hadn't found her and threw some more snow before giving up.

"I know you're here somewhere," said Brian. Lilly didn't respond and stayed very quiet. "Fine, you can take the gem this time, but don't think you'll always get so lucky." With that, he continued walking toward her tour group, and Lilly continued following stealthily behind.

9: Where Have You Been?

Lilly reached the tour group and snuck through the crowd, still invisible. She found Peter and their parents, who looked worried. They seemed to be searching for something, or someone. She heard her mom ask Becky if she had seen Lilly, and Lilly felt a little guilty about running off. She decided it was safe to become visible again.

How did she make herself visible again? She only knew how to activate the gem's powers, but not how to deactivate them. Lilly decided to try to imagine herself visible again. She closed her eyes and willed herself to be seen.

"There you are," said her dad's voice behind her. Lilly opened her eyes and turned around to see her mom running towards her with Peter following behind with an apologetic look.

"Where have you been?" asked her dad.

"I got lost in the crowd," said Lilly, slipping the gem into her coat pocket. She knew there was no way out of trouble no matter what she said.

"Your mom and I have been very worried," said her dad.

"First, Peter slips on ice and hurts himself, then you disappear. Are you two trying to give me a heart attack?" asked their mom, very clearly upset and worried. It seemed like Peter's distraction hadn't worked quite as well as he had said it would.

"I'm sorry," said Lilly. "I wanted to ask Becky something but couldn't find her."

"She was helping us after Peter fell," said her mom, a little skeptically. Lilly could tell that her parents were going to be watching her even more closely.

"Is Peter okay?" asked Lilly, trying to change the subject.

"I'm a bit bruised up, but other than that I'm fine," answered Peter.

"Come on, we're going," said her mom, not interested in the change of topic.

"Where are we going?" asked Lilly, a little confused.

"Back to our hotel for the rest of the day, so that way you can't get lost again," replied her mom.

With that, they all headed back to their hotel, where Lilly and her dad spent the rest of the day while Peter and their mom went shopping. Her dad worked on writing his article while Lilly just sat around reading one of the books she brought. Since they couldn't sight-see, her mom had decided to at least get some more souvenirs. Lilly was grounded, so she couldn't join them, but Peter made sure to get her a terracotta soldier figurine.

Her parents were still upset, but they didn't have to cancel their plans, since they were leaving the next day anyways.

10: Grounded

Later that day, Lilly told Peter about what had happened.

"Wait, so you actually used the gem to create a shield around you, and to make yourself invisible?" asked Peter, seeming shocked by this revelation.

"Yes," said Lilly. "Though we need to discuss the next gem."

"Did you find anything about it?" asked Peter.

"No," admitted Lilly. "Where are we going next again?"

"I think it was Macho Pancho or something," said Peter.

"Machu Picchu," said Lilly.

"Well, that's assuming Mom and Dad let us go," said Peter. "They might not if you keep disappearing like that."

"We both disappeared at Petra," Lilly reminded him.

"It was your idea," Peter argued as if this made any difference. "Anyway, I was correct about this gem was I not?"

"I guess your sources weren't as invalid as I thought," said Lilly reluctantly. "What do you know about Machu Picchu? Are there any gems there?"

"I only looked up the Great Wall of China," said Peter. "I'll see if Mom and Dad will let me look it up when we get home. Since you're grounded."

"You don't have to rub it in since it was your job to distract them," said Lilly.

"You shouldn't have taken so long," said Peter.

"I ran into Brian on my way back, so I'm sorry if I wasn't fast enough," replied Lilly. "Next time I'll just give him the gem and hurry back then." Peter didn't seem to have a comeback to this, so Lilly changed the subject before he could think of one. "Anyway, are you going to try using the *Ageless Gem* when we get home?"

"What would I do with it, make it so we live forever?" asked Peter sarcastically. "Its powers aren't quite as flashy as the *Gem of Protection*."

"Then I guess you'll have to wait for the next gem to try out any cool powers," said Lilly.

"If we ever get a chance to get the next gem," said Peter.

Lilly sighed, Peter had a point. Hopefully, their parents would still allow them to go to Machu Picchu with them. They were still pretty upset about Lilly disappearing, so she was still unsure about whether they would let her go or not. Lilly would have to try and find some way to convince her parents to let her go to Machu Picchu, for she had a feeling that was where the next gem was.

11: Dumplings, Ducks, and Brian?

The next day their dad took Peter to the Ming Tombs while Lilly had to stay at the hotel with their mom. Her mom decided that they shouldn't sit around all day bored. They were still on vacation after all. Lilly promised to stay close and to hold her mom's hand, so the two of them went to a nearby restaurant.

The restaurant offered foods Lilly had never seen before. There were dumplings, Beijing roast duck, and many other things she had never even heard of before. Lilly found it somewhat interesting how different the food was from what she was used to.

Lilly and her mom both tried the shredded pork in Beijing sauce, and the Chinese dumplings. The pork was sweet and the dumplings were warm and steaming.

"Is it good?" asked her mom. Lilly nodded her head and smiled. "Well, I'm glad I did some research ahead of time."

"What do you mean?" asked Lilly.

"Before we came on the trip I did some research on what kind of foods are common here," explained her mom. "It's always a good idea to do a little research into the cuisine of a foreign place before you visit. Even if you're just going sightseeing, you still need to eat at some point, and it's better to know what you're eating so you don't get surprised by something unexpected." Her mom laughed a little as if to a private joke.

Lilly had never thought of that before. Though she had never really considered food to be an important thing to think about when traveling to see famous structures. Maybe she should do more research on the local cuisine of their future destinations.

As they walked back to the hotel Lilly saw a familiar face. Brian. What was he doing here? Brian looked right at Lilly. Still holding her mother's hand, she pulled out the necklace from beneath her coat. She squeezed it in her hand and attempted to make her and her mom invisible. There was a tingling sensation as she felt the magic envelope her. As this happened a crisp cold wind blew, and she felt her mom shiver slightly.

When she opened her eyes she saw that Brian seemed very surprised and upset, and paired with the slight glow around her, she assumed she had succeeded. However, Lilly suddenly realized something. What if her mom noticed something was wrong? What if she noticed the slight glow in the air around them? What if she felt Lilly making them invisible? What if—

Lilly's thoughts were cut off by her mom. "Is it just me or did that wind feel weird?"

"I don't know," said Lilly in a bit of a panic. "Let's hurry back to the hotel. Peter and dad should be back soon, right?"

"We're already heading back to the hotel," said her mom, sounding a little confused.

"Oh, I thought the hotel was the other way," said Lilly, looking around and seeing Brian walking in their direction. Lilly realized that even if he didn't know where they were, he still knew the general direction they were heading in.

They entered the hotel behind a group of people, so Brian ended up walking right past. Much to Lilly's relief. It also seemed her mother hadn't noticed the invisibility. Maybe only Lilly could see the slight glow since she summoned the powers, or maybe because she was one of the gem masters? Lilly concentrated and removed the magic surrounding her and her mom, making them both visible again. There was a slight tingling sensation as the magic fell away. Her mother seemed to notice this as she frowned slightly and looked around.

"Did you feel that?" asked her mom.

"Feel what?" asked Lilly, feigning ignorance.

"Nevermind," said her mom, shaking her head.

12: Machu Picchu, Here We Come!

Lilly was unable to tell Peter about the day's events that night, but she did hear her mom mention that she thought the hotel might be haunted.

However, the next day on the airplane Lilly was able to tell Peter about what happened. Peter also told her about his uneventful visit to the Ming Tombs. Apparently, nothing had caught his eye as important or interesting.

"Wish I could have been with you guys," said Peter. "The tour was so boring. Especially without someone asking questions about magical gems at random points during the tour."

"Did you not try to ask questions to find out more about the gems?" asked Lilly.

"It didn't seem like there was anything to learn," said Peter. "I don't think the tour guide knew anything about the gems. There wasn't anything that seemed related to the gems there anyways."

"You could have still asked," Lilly pointed out.

"Whatever," said Peter. "I'm the one doing research on the next gem anyways. Since you're grounded and all."

"Do you want me to spell out Machu Picchu for you?" asked Lilly. "That way you can make sure you research the right place."

"Very funny," said Peter. "I'm sure I'll be able to figure it out just fine."

"Sure," Lilly teased him.

A few days later Lilly was looking through the books on her bookshelf when Peter appeared in her doorway. He seemed to be excited.

"The next gem is said to be hidden at Machu Picchu," Peter said excitedly. "And it's not something lame like the *Ageless Gem*."

"What is the next gem called then?" asked Lilly, happy that her theory was correct. She glanced over to the jewelry box on her dresser where she had hidden the necklace with the *Gem of Protection.*

"It's supposedly called the *Gem of Water*," said Peter. "Do you think I'll get this one? I really want to try out some of the gems' powers."

"Can't you use the *Gem of Age*?" asked Lilly.

"Yeah, but those powers aren't as cool," said Peter. "Plus it's not like those powers will help me fend off Brian like you did."

"Well I guess you're not wrong about that," said Lilly.

"So now that we know this, is there anything else I should try to research before our next trip?" asked Peter.

Lilly thought for a minute before replying, "Try to see if there are any theories as to where the gem might be hidden." Then after a short pause. "Also can you look into the local cuisine of Peru?"

Peter gave her a curious look, but nodded

and said, "I'll have to look into it another day. Dad has to work on his article right now, so he's going to be using the computer."

"Okay, but make sure you remember," said Lilly.

"Why would I forget?" asked Peter.

"I don't know," said Lilly teasingly. "But if you do I'll remind you."

"Whatever," said Peter as he left her alone.

Lilly smiled as she selected a book about the seven wonders of the world, and opened it to Machu Picchu. She was right, the next gem was at Machu Picchu. Now Lilly needed to do as much research as she could on Machu Picchu.

Looking over to her bookshelf again; Lilly thought she might ask her parents for a Peru travel guide. That way she could be as prepared as possible for their trip to Machu Picchu. That was, if she could still go.

Acknowledgements

Thank you to everyone who's helped me to achieve my dream of being an author. I want to thank my family for supporting me and for helping me through the publishing process. I want to thank my friends at school, some of which are also aspiring authors. My teachers too, who were all excited about my books.

I want to thank the team at TouchPoint Press for allowing me this opportunity to publish my books.

Are you new Raeann Gillberg's series?

Grab book one: *The Ageless Gem*
for more exciting adventures!

Peter and his family are visiting Petra, a very old structure carved out of a cliff in Jordan and one of the seven wonders of the world. But for Peter this is anything besides a normal family vacation. From Peter's strange dreams to Lilly's crazy theories, nothing seems to make sense. Will Peter look past what he thinks he knows and find something inside himself he didn't know was there? Will he unravel the mystery of the Ageless Gem, or is it nothing more than an ageless bedtime story?

Made in the USA
Monee, IL
21 November 2022

18240735R00031